DIVING AND SNORKELING GUIDE TO

Bali
and The Komodo Region

Tim Rock

 Pisces Books®

🜨 Pisces Books®

Copyright © 1996 by Lonely Planet Publications

Head Office: PO Box 617, Hawthorn, Vic 3122, Australia
Branches: 155 Filbert St, Suite 251, Oakland, CA 94607, USA
10a Spring Place, London NW5 3BH, UK
71 bis rue du Cardinal Lemoine, 75005 Paris, France

Printed in Hong Kong.

Library of Congress Cataloging-in-Publication Data

Rock, Tim.
    Diving and snorkeling guide to Bali and the Komodo Region /
Tim Rock.
       p. cm.
    Includes index.
    ISBN 1-55992-086-6
    1. Deep diving—Indonesia—Bali Island—Guidebooks. 2. Skin
diving—Indonesia—Bali Island—Guidebooks. 3. Bali Island
(Indonesia)—Guidebooks. I. Title.
GV840.S78R5715 1996
797.2′3′095986—dc20   95-31242
                                  CIP

Table of Contents

Preface

The island of Bali is a magical place.

There are few cultures more revered in the world than that of the Balinese. Their ancient tales are acted out through vibrant plays and colorful costumes from the religion that governs their lives. Music and incense constantly fill the air as the day and night are a celebration of the Hindu way of life. Bali is known throughout the world for its art, for its gentle people, and for its beautiful volcanic scenery accented everywhere by rolling green rice paddies.

Three million people live here, more than half around the tourist areas like Kuta and Sanur. Denpasar is a huge Balinese population center of more than a million. It is surrounded by the Indian Ocean and the Java Sea. To get to the diving sites, a ride along the highway to the northeast is in order and is somewhat like an amusement park ride. Bikes, motorcycles, cars, trucks, buses, and big transports all vie for space along the roads here. The general rule is the largest vehicle has the right-of-way, which can make for some interesting and, at times, white-knuckled kilometers of driving.

The east coast is truly beautiful, with rice paddies stretching for miles. Outside of the city, farming is the major profession. Life is lived along the roadside, and the Balinese culture can be seen as people live their lives in the sun.

How to Use This Guide

This guide is intended to bring to the diver the most popular and unique dive sites of Bali and the islands in the Nusa Tengarra region, places known for their wide variety of beautiful invertebrates, sponges, hard and soft corals, and unusual sea life. Approximate dive positions are shown on the maps of each region. In addition, each site is introduced with a chart that tells general location, most frequently dived depths, type of dive that can be expected, the dominant marine life, and the logistical requirements. Bali has about a million tourists, many of whom are introductory divers. This book has included a variety of sites from the best snorkeling reefs to beach dives to the more exciting boat dives. The more experienced, traveling diver also comes to Bali for the rich photographic experiences, unique sea life and wild current rides. These must-see dives also are listed, all of which easily can be done with a boat and resident guide. The reefs of Bali are truly spectacular. They are fitting for a country known for its beauty and art, and are worth preserving and protecting for future divers to see and admire.

The Rating System for Divers and Dives

The Levels: *Novice* is considered someone who is in decent physical condition, who is newly certified or who dives infrequently, or who is not experienced with ocean diving. *Advanced* is considered someone with advanced training who dives frequently and is comfortable with ocean diving. *Expert* is considered someone at divemaster or instructor level who is in excellent shape. Two things conspire against the diver in Micronesia: incredible clarity and strong currents. You will have to be alert for changing conditions and to monitor depth closely. Please consider before making every dive the way you feel that particular day, your level of training, physical condition, and water conditions at the site. It is no sin to abort a dive. Remember the adage: There are old divers and there are bold divers, but there aren't many old, bold divers. Be honest in evaluating your diving skills.

1

Overview of Bali

The People

There are but a few who visit Bali who don't fall in love with the charm of the Balinese people. To these resident Balinese, religion and lifestyle are one. Their openness, charm, and curiosity make them the perfect hosts. About three million people live on Bali. Denpasar is the largest city. It is located in the south and features modern shopping centers, huge art and craft markets, and lots of two-wheeled vehicles.

A Kuta Beach massage is a must in Bali.

◀ *Soft leather corals carpet the sea floor at Crystal Bay offshore Bali at southwestern Nusa Penida island.*

Public transportation is excellent on Bali. You can cross the city or the island cheaply, or travel to many adjoining islands and cultures for very little. If you plan to dive and travel, it is best to do your diving and then travel, as public transport can be very crowded and room for extra gear sparse. Or you can rent a *bemo* (van) and driver by the day or week and travel with someone who speaks the language. This is a negotiable item but can be an interesting way to see the country.

Car rental is available, and an auto excursion from south to east and from north to west can bring many memorable experiences and views of some varied and awe-inspiring terrain. Remember to drive defensively, stay away from alcohol, and avoid driving at night if at all possible. These tips should keep you out of trouble on the wacky, but always interesting Bali byways and highways.

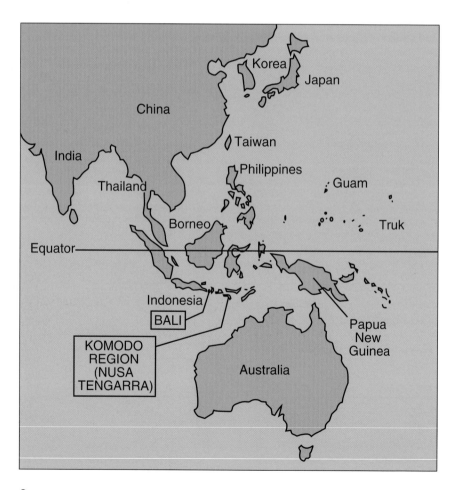

Accommodations and Conditions

Bali has something for every taste and budget. Five-star, first-class hotels can be found lining the beach in Sanur. Just a few miles away, a beach-side rustic, family-owned cottage in Legian may go for just a few dollars daily. There are *losmen* all over Bali. These are considered simple, local accommodations where the *rakyat* (local population) prefers to stay. Most are run by families, and the quality of your stay in Bali may depend on the *losmen*. Look for one that is well-cared for, away from the highway noise, and away from anything that breeds mosquitoes. Most are made of natural material like bamboo and decorated by flowers and Balinese art figures. Hot tea and a couple of bananas are normally sitting at your front patio early every morn.

Balinese do not, on the whole, travel nearly as much as their visitors, so they are friendly and curious. They are also anxious to practice their Eng-

At Tulamben, women carry tanks down the beach on their heads.

Bougainvilleas line a homefront in Tulamben.

lish, which may be spoken with an Australian accent. You may find your-self answering a pretty standard set of questions quite often. Do not be impatient. They are genuinely trying to be curious and sociable. If their English is good and they can carry on a conversation, you will find theirs is a fascinating culture. Listen and learn.

Outside of the tourist centers, few speak much more than a few words of English, even in the city. So, it is best to carry a small phrase book to get your food ordered or to obtain your always-necessary bottled water.

A giant barrel sponge sits on the Liberty ship at Tulamben.

Nature and Wildlife

The island of Bali has an exotic array of flora and fauna even though it boasts a population of approximately three million. The heavily populated areas give way to large rural tracts that are used mainly for rice cultivation. The many high volcanic mountains also provide growth areas for forest tracts that are habitat for many reptiles, insects, and birds.

In fact, Indonesia's bird species number in the thousands, and Bali has many rare and endemic birds. For frequent guided birdwatching tours to the rice paddies and forest lands, see the Beggar's Bush Inn in Ubud, strong supporters of Audubon activity.

The vast western peninsula of the island, as well as the small island of Menjangen at its tip, has designated reserves and protected areas that are home to deer and monkeys. The deer have even been spotted swimming across the peninsula to Menjangen (which means deer in Balinese). This island is a preserve that is home to a rare Balinese bird (*seng ken ken*) and occasionally the deer herd. The reefs around the island are varied and spectacular.

There are no odd monsters—like Komodo dragons—on the island. In fact, Bali is believed to be where the split took place that separated the islands and Australia. The animals found in Bali have few cousins just across the channel on Lombok Island. The animal life from Lombok south and east in Indonesia is distinctly like that inhabiting the Australian continent. The animals west of Bali and on Bali are common to Asia.

There are more than 2,500 species of fish found in the Indonesian waters, and many are found off the shore of Bali. This is one of the richest areas in the world for marine creatures.

The invertebrate life and corals are equally diverse. These waters are a picnic for the macrophotographer as the coloration of the sedentary animals is splendid, ranging from bright oranges, reds, and yellows to subtle pastels and electric shades of blue.

◀ *Crinoids sit near a brain coral at S.D.*

The morning mist spreads along the morning sea in Lovina. ▶

2

Diving Bali

Amed Dropoff   1

Location:	Northeast Bali
Attractions:	Corals, tons of small fish
Depth:	20 to 90 feet
Logistics:	Shore dive
Level:	Snorkel, novice, advanced, expert

Not quite as far as the Kubu Dropoff is the undersea slope at Amed. This site is found just as you get out of the scenic mountains and rice terraces and enter the plains of the Amed region. There is a short hike along the shore involved in getting down to the beach entry here.

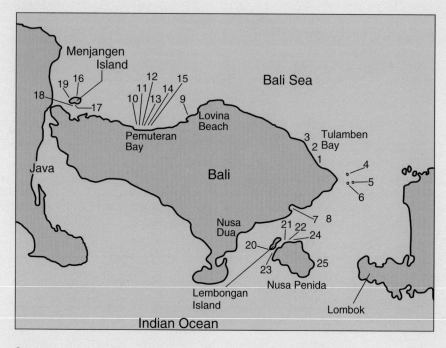

Dive Site Ratings

		Snorkel	Novice	Advanced	Expert
Bali					
1	Amed Dropoff	x	x	x	x
2	Kubu Corner	x	x	x	x
3	Liberty Shipwreck	x	x	x	x
4	Ikuan Island			x	x
5	Kambing Island			x	x
6	Gili Topekang			x	x
7	Padang Bai East		x	x	x
8	Padang Bai West		x	x	x
9	Lovina Beach	x	x	x	x
10	Napoleon Reef	x	x	x	x
11	Close Encounters	x	x	x	x
12	Lebar Reef			x	x
13	Temple Wall	x	x	x	x
14	Kebun Batu	x	x	x	x
15	Kebun Chris	x	x	x	x
16	Menjangen North	x	x	x	x
17	Menjangen South	x	x	x	x
18	Menjangen Channel	x	x	x	x
19	Menjangen Slopes	x	x	x	x
20	Lembongan Marine Park	x	x	x	x
21	Blue Corner			x	x
22	Sekolah Desar (S.D.)	x	x	x	x
23	Mangrove Point	x	x	x	x
24	Crystal Bay	x	x	x	x
25	Manta Point	x	x	x	x

The surrounding terrain shows less of the volcanic activity that rocked the coastline farther north near Tulamben. The water here is also generally calm most of the year, with currents manageable to minimal.

The true attraction here is the fish life as opposed to the corals so prevalent along the popular eastern sites, but that doesn't mean the site is sparse. There is a sort of ledge region that incorporates itself with the gradual dropoff of the terrain. This is in the 30 to 40 foot depths and features white sand patches with coral heads and staghorn corals.

These staghorns are the homes of immense schools of aquarium fish. The diversity defies in-depth description, but there are butterflyfishes, including the brilliant yellow long-nosed butterflyfish; angelfishes, including the majestic emperor angelfish and the regal angelfish; and basslets, blennies, chromis and damsels.

There are also various schools of fish like sapphire yellowtails and blue-streak fusiliers that course the reef and occasionally surround the diver in movement and color.

Joining the active fish schools on the reef are lots of moray eels that seem to like this spot, perhaps for the abundant fish life that doubles as a meal for the toothy critters. The diver should take care when poking his hand into a crevice for a shell or some other goody. It may be occupied by a moray that could react negatively to the intrusion.

The slope descends to sponges and fan corals along the deeper regions of the dropoff. There is also a mini-wall that drops to about 90 feet and has some interesting nooks and crevices full of clear baitfish. The trip back up into the mountain region is a quick one from Amed, so dives here should be shallow. The trip to the surface can add one full stop or more to your dive profile and must be taken into account for safe decompression.

Kubu Corner

Location:	Tulamben Bay
Attractions:	Sponges, sea fans, fish
Depth:	5 to 100 feet
Logistics:	Shore dive
Level:	Snorkel, novice, advanced, expert

Bali's exotic aura extends into its ocean realm. Kubu Dropoff is located on the northeast shore of the Badung Strait. To get there from Kuta, an early morning start takes you out of the city and tourist areas and into the

---

The Lionfish

Sometimes they're called lionfish, sometimes turkeyfish; the Australians even label them butterfly cod. They're one of the most spectacular-looking fishes on the reef. They're also one of the most poisonous. Divers are attracted to this fish out of curiosity and respect. It is, at times, a wonder how any animal so beautiful can also be so deadly. They are bold and seem to advertise their presence. It can be seen hovering over the reef in search of food, its flowing fins extended. One good place to find them is Kubu Dropoff as the sun gets low. Once a lionfish finds an area it likes, it can be located there consistently for years. Usually found hiding under coral outcrops or ledges, often upside down, the animal can be gently coaxed into the open for photos and observation. It will do its best to retreat and only attack when provoked or panicked. But if it turns to face its attacker and lays back its fins with its head down at a 45 degree angle, beware. That display means it has had enough of being a spectacle and is ready for business.

◄ *Coral staghorn forests layer the upper reef at Amed.*

rural countryside. Balinese rise early, around 5 a.m., so villages are a flurry of activity and everything in Bali happens on the street. The sights, sounds and smells make the time pass and provide a good look into daily life here. Or stay closer by in Candi Dasa or even Tulamben village for a later rising time.

The terrain winds through a variety of locales including beautifully terraced rice paddies, past the majestic volcano Agung and through a wasteland of towering pandanas trees. The road skirts the coastline and stops in a small village of wood and thatched houses. From nowhere come various-sized equipment porters of all ages. A short walk past multicolored outriggers brings the diver to a black, rocky beach. After suiting up, the entry is quite simple, and a gradual descent is made while swimming around a rocky point. Clouds of chromis and fluorescent basslets glitter the reeftop. Gorgonians sway gently. Large batfish and angels knife through the water.

Perhaps the most striking aspects of the dive are the huge sponges. Big barrel sponges large enough for a diver to sit in and stands of purple tube sponges add form and color to an already alive reef. Nearby, anemones with clown anemonefish and Peterson shrimp feed in the rich water.

Coming out of the water, a hillside Hindu temple stands watch over Tulamben Bay, dwarfed by a looming distant volcano. Visibility here can be low during rainy season, but the runoff feeds the immense sponges, so it is a good trade-off. This is also a great dusk or night dive, with more lionfish to the square inch than you can imagine.

Tiny Tulamben village is becoming more developed for diving. ▶

◀ *Sea fans line the mini-wall at Kubu Dropoff.*

Liberty Shipwreck   3

Location:	Tulamben Shore
Attractions:	Coral-covered U.S. Liberty ship
Depth:	20 to 90 feet
Logistics:	Shore dive
Level:	Snorkel, novice, advanced, expert

Along the coast near tiny Tulamben village, there is an attraction that lots of divers visit every day. Off this arid stretch of land lined with cactus and pandanas, an American ship rests just below the surface. The arrival of divers means excitement. With seemingly no effort, porters, both men and women of all ages, carry gear, tanks, and cameras down the rocky beach. The head is the favorite place to transport a tank!

This ship has become a natural reef, attracting some of the most colorful fish in the Indo-Pacific.

The ship was a victim of World War II. It is the American ship USAT Liberty, an armed cargo steamship damaged by the Japanese in 1942. It is large and somewhat broken up, sitting on a black sand shelf that slopes from about 20 feet to 90.

A bumphead parrot hovers over the Liberty wreck, munching bits of coral.

◀ *Giant vase sponges sit on the reef at Kubu Dropoff.*

Fish feeding is a popular activity at the Liberty ship.

Her demise came when she was torpedoed by a Japanese submarine on the 11th of January in 1942. She was in the straits about ten miles southwest of Lombok. Two American destroyers, the HNMS Van Ghent and the USS Paul Jones, came to her rescue and towed her toward Bali. Her damage was extensive, so the crew was evacuated and she was beached. The Americans had the intention of returning to salvage her and her contents, which was raw rubber and railroad parts, among other things.

The war escalated and that never happened. She sat beached, pretty much intact and visible along this pristine coast until Mt. Agung blew its stack in 1963. It toppled beneath the water during that extremely violent eruption. She lies parallel to the beach with her bow pointing to the north. The stern is somewhat intact, the midship is in a shambles, and the bow is in pretty good shape. It is a big wreck, perhaps 400 feet long. It was built in 1915.

This ship is covered with an incredible variety of coral and marine life. The Java Sea is one of the most diverse in the world, and invertebrate life is profuse. This has to be one of the most colorful wrecks in the world.

As it is a popular tourist dive, fish feeding keeps a large resident population of hungry tangs and other reef tropicals around. They will smother the diver while trying to get some morsels of food.

16

The ship is a haven for emperators and aggressive batfish. Some guides feed the fish here, so they are tame and good photo subjects.

Huge gorgonians, sponges and corals also have grown on the ship. This extremely rich coral growth is mostly the product of the past 25 years or so, so it is easy to see how abundant the marine life is in this part of the world. There are a number of portholes still intact, and if the local guides have their way, they will remain intact. Poking around in the sand for a safety stop also can be fun. There are spotted stingrays here that like to munch just below the sea floor looking for small shrimps and other such critters.

One warning: Lots of divers visit this site, normally between the hours of 9 a.m. and 3 p.m., so stay nearby and dive early or late if you don't like crowds.

A baby green sea turtle makes its way along the shallow rocks.

Ikuan Island 4

Location:	Gili Biaha Point
Attractions:	Sponges, crinoids, schools of fish
Depth:	25 to 130 feet
Logistics:	Boat dive
Level:	Advanced, expert

Ikuan Island is a rocky outcrop located just off a point called Gili Biaha, perhaps a mile or more north of Kambing Island. The west side of the island is the preferred site here. This island slopes gradually to well over 120 feet in the strait between the Bali mainland and the island. The slope itself offers a great variety of fish life. Depending on the seas and tides, there can be an incredible current running along the slope. Crinoids will be found in great numbers attached to the tops of large barrel sponges. They will sometimes be bent by the current.

There are many trigger and surgeonfish in the area. Fish also let this current bring them food particles. Many species can be seen bobbing up and down catching tidbits as they wash by. This current also brings around the large schools of the brilliant blue yellowtail fusiliers. These fish are as curious as they are abundant. If you stop and wait, chances are the school will swim around you so close that the fish can nearly be touched. This is a great sensation and sometimes ends as quickly as it started, so be alert and prepared to take advantage of the experience.

At Ikuan Island, yellow fusiliers appear in large schools.

Table corals and reef tropicals are prolific at Gili Topekang. ▶

Encrusting invertebrates give variety and color to the rocks and reef.

Currents are strong here, and coral life is not thick. Yet there are large sea fans along this slope, including beautiful gorgonians with snowy white polyps and blood red skeletons. There are also large coral heads that provide shelter against the current and allow the diver to duck in and look around at the marine life making its home in the cracks and crevices along Ikuan. The invertebrate life is very plentiful. There can be some really tricky current action at times, with up-and-down currents coming with horizontal jetstreams to really give a ride. That is why this is rated an advanced dive, as a less experienced diver may feel uncomfortable or have a tendency to panic if not used to equalizing and handling these situations of odd sensations.

However, it can also be calm as a lake here.

There are more corals in the shallow depths, and pelagic animals like tunas and sharks also have been seen at Ikuan.

Location:	Off Candi Dasa coast
Attractions:	Tunnel, corals, pelagics
Depth:	30 to 100 feet
Logistics:	Boat dive
Level:	Advanced, expert

Kambing Island, also called Pulau Kambing, is a volcanic hump rising out of the water north of the Badung Strait. A three-mile boat ride from Buitan or an even shorter hop from Candi Dasa will put the diver in an area of submerged peaks that form a broken reef.

This area is covered with Medusalike heads that vary greatly in size from huge boulders to small sea gardens. They are adorned with blood-red

The Candi Dasa coast is a haven for local fishermen.

Incredible colors dot the Kambing Island reef, like this bluetip table coral.

sea fans, tunicates, and various sponges. In other spots, the competition for space among the corals is incredible. There are areas where a diver cannot rest on the bottom for fear of damaging the thick coral growth.

Near the island, the bottom appears at about 40 feet and slopes gently well past 100. Kambing is often regarded as a drift dive as strong currents develop during tide changes. A Kambing drift dive can take the diver along the island's wall, which is frequented by a lot of fish . . . big ones.

Golden jacks and huge batfish swim in the open water while bigeyes and some incredibly colorful groupers take up the cracks and the crevices. Blue lobsters are also in some holes. On one dive, we were greeted by five whitetip sharks—two of which were well over six feet long—when we entered the water on the north side of Kambing. One curious shark stayed with us throughout the dive, probably looking for a speared fish handout. It is believed the whitetips rest during the day in the caves and holes near the boulders along the western edge of the island.

Currents flush the water and keep it clear, enhancing visibility. They also bring some pretty cool water up from the depths. A tropical diver can get downright cold here without a wetsuit. This is called an advanced dive because of the strong currents that occasionally develop here, but the west side of the island is generally manageable most of the time.

22

Gili Topekang 6

Location:	Near Pulau Kambing
Attractions:	Coral gardens, resting sharks
Depth:	10 to 80 feet
Logistics:	Boat dive
Level:	Advanced, expert

These are the small islands closer to shore near Kambing Island. They are home to garudas—ocean eagles—who nest here and then fly over the waves at dawn in search of fish. There is good diving here, with whitetip sharks that like to sleep in the current-swept flats.

The sea fans along the fringing reef of the islands and their channels must have a good dozen crinoids per sea fan. Some are incredibly colorful, with brilliant red sea fans being adorned by sea spiders of yellow, black, and forest green.

Magnificent angelfish and clouds of chromis mix with crimson basslets and schools of yellowtails. Napoleon wrasse are frequently spotted, and there have been large gray reef sharks seen coming in from the deep.

A sea star adorns the reef at Gili Topekang.

A crinoid sits on a sponge in the rich channel along Gili Topekang.

This place really does not get the diving following it deserves, possibly because of the tricky currents. But these currents and ocean upwellings support planktonic life that attracts animals like whale sharks, which have been seen in the waters between Gili Topekang and Kambing. Eagle rays and large black rays also are found near the Gilis, as are lanky leopard sharks.

There is a large school of Moorish idols that is a very colorful photo subject. The idols are deeper near the outer dropoff. Diving is usually made in kind of a circular pattern, going with a current that flows around the rocky islands and back to the boat. It averages only about 60 feet or less here, so plenty of time can be taken to enjoy the area.

Padang Bai East 7

Location:	Near Padang Bai village
Attractions:	Coral gardens
Depth:	10 to 80 feet
Logistics:	Boat dive
Level:	Novice, advanced, expert

Padang Bai is a port area for the Lombok ferry, which docks here many times daily. The shallow reefs nearby are used for introductory dives, night dives, and long photo excursions. Just around the tip near the point, there is a beautiful sandy beach. Staghorn coral patch reefs start in only ten feet of water. The reef then opens to a diverse area with brain corals,

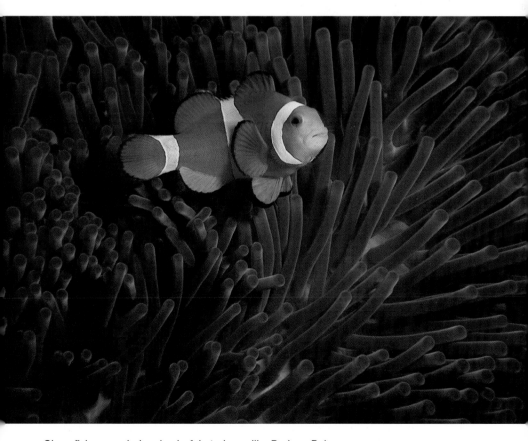

Clownfish are varied and colorful at places like Padang Bai.

Candelabra sponges are adorned with golden crinoids.

soft corals, and flowing leather coral. The delicate plate corals here are well-developed and have hints of color like fringes of purple and blue.

Bali's exceptional invertebrate life can be seen here. A wide variety of Christmas tree worms in all sizes and colors poke from the rocks and coral heads. The small damsels and basslets seem to never stop moving, and butterflyfish are in abundance.

For those more experienced, there is a wall of sorts at about 80 feet. Please note that down currents have been experienced here and care should be taken by those making a deeper dive. Start deep and work your way back up the wall to the coral gardens for the best of both worlds.

Padang Bai West 8

Location:	Near Padang Bai village
Attractions:	Varied marine life
Depth:	30 to 100 feet
Logistics:	Boat dive
Level:	Novice, advanced, expert

Opposite the Padang Bai east shore dive, the terrain here is markedly different from the coral-laden bottom across the bay. Rocky boulders host corals and invertebrates. The leather corals here are quite large, resembling sea anemones as their extended polyps feed in the currents.

There is a sandy shore, and some staghorn thickets are here as well. Groupers, angelfish, feathery lionfish, and tropicals fill out the smaller end of the marine spectrum. Larger marine life is found on this dive, like gray reef sharks, stingrays, and schools of small, silvery tuna and mackerel.

This site also is known to have large cuttlefish that like to interact with divers. These big squid make pulsing color changes and can be approached quite closely if the diver keeps his or her movements slow and even so as not to spook the curious fish.

More than 90 types of crinoids in varied colors inhabit the reefs of Bali.

Location:	North Central Bali
Attractions:	Reef fish and corals
Depth:	2 to 70 feet
Logistics:	Boat snorkel or dive
Level:	Snorkel, novice, advanced expert

   The northern coastal resorts of Bali are a real departure from the upbeat Kuta scene. Most are small and exude a laid-back atmosphere that seems to attract the budget-minded and non-conforming.

   The beaches here are dark and volcanic, and are littered with merchants and topless swimmers by day. Colorful jukungs, the outriggers with the triangular sails, have captains who will rise early for a snorkel or dive trip.

   The water is still glassy at 6 or 7 a.m., and a mist rises off the still ocean. Colorful sails and their vivid reflections dance off the sea as outrigger blades cut quietly through the water.

   Snorkeling here is quite pleasant, with large schools of silver chromis. Bright yellow and dappled crinoids sit atop odd stands of fire coral and acropora feeding in the gentle currents. Beautiful butterflyfish scurry for cover in the coral crevices and crannies as snorkelers pass overhead. There are also encrusting sponges and varied corals. It is a pleasant way to start the day and greet Mother Ocean.

At Lovina, bright crinoids can be seen by snorkelers.

Location:	Northwest Bali
Attractions:	Large sponges, fans, fusiliers
Depth:	15 to 130 feet
Logistics:	Boat dive
Level:	All levels

All of the reefs in this area have been developed by Chris Brown of the Reef Seen Dive Centre in Pemuteran Bay. Brown's love for the ocean has seen the establishment of a turtle nesting program, a stoppage of aquarium fish collecting, and the aiding of reef-building corals to re-establish themselves in damaged areas. Brown has a sharp eye when it comes to invertebrate life and can be a very valuable dive buddy for a photographer or nature buff.

Named for a large Napoleon wrasse seen here, this great little reef has it all. It can be dived deep or shallow, day or night. On the northeast end

Watching cuttlefish is fascinating once you know where their nesting area is at the southeast end of Napoleon Reef.

A diver is surrounded by tiny fish while videotaping a leaf fish at Napoleon Reef.

of the reef is the ikan warung, fish house, where there are schools of fish all over. Golden sea fans and large clumps of cotton candy coral grow with other gorgonians along the slope. Take a turn around the east end of the reef and head south and large barrel sponges over five feet high and three feet in diameter are found. Crinoids like to sit on their outer edges while damsels sometimes hover inside.

Sea Turtles

The sea turtle is one of the most fascinating creatures in the ocean to observe. The reason for this is their powerful, yet graceful, way of swimming in the sea. With seemingly effortless movements, they soar into the blue water of the ocean dropoffs. Mesmerized, divers may follow, only later to find the sea turtle has led them on a merry chase into the depths. Turtles were hunted in Bali, but many are making efforts to stop this as they are an endangered species. Given time to grow, sea turtles can become very large. With age and size come wisdom. The turtle will let a diver come just so close, then, with a couple of powerful strokes, disappear into the abyss.

The coral gardens in the shallows along this rich reef area are spectacular, with large platter corals growing one atop the other for a beautiful layered scene. These are in only 20 feet of water and can be snorkeled as well as dived.

Chris Brown uses this reef to observe cuttlefish and can predict their egg-laying behavior. Watching them is fascinating once you know where their nesting area is at the southeast end of Napoleon Reef. The cuttlefish are wary of divers, but they can't resist the urge to plant their eggs, which are placed in the protective branches of fire coral. They will move up to the coral head and extend their long tentacles way out into a funnel. All of a sudden, a small, soft egg sack pops out and glues itself to the the coral. The cuttlefish will continue this act for hours until the inner branches of the coral head are filled with egg sacks.

Trumpetfish—especially the odd bright-yellow ones with a symbiotic jack following, yellow jacks, gray snappers, rainbow runners, and an occasional barracuda all like to join the myriad chromis and basslets here to feed in the light current. Large fusilier schools and a good variety of starfish are commonly seen on this dive.

The coral gardens in the shallows along Napoleon Reef are spectacular, with large platter corals growing one atop the other for a beautiful layered scene.

Close Encounters   11

Location:	Northwest Bali
Attractions:	Short dropoff, garden eels
Depth:	10 to 120 feet
Logistics:	Boat dive
Level:	All levels

Close Encounters has been called such because manta rays sometimes are seen here. And, a pure white manta is reported to be in the area and occasionally is seen, making a close encounter with these gentle and graceful ocean giants special. But hang on, that's not all. This place can

Soft corals in pastel hues are especially impressive at Close Encounters.

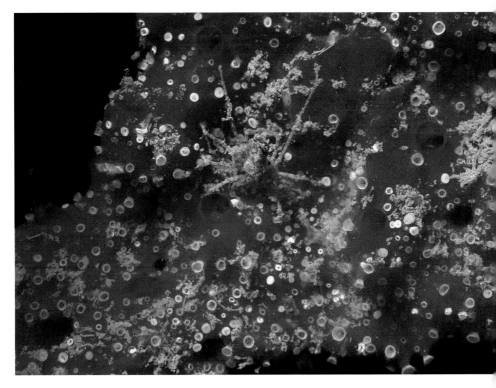

An arrow crab seeks camouflage at Close Encounters.

be totally unpredictable. Whale sharks have been spotted during the planktonic months from December through April, but can show at any time. Whales have been seen spouting very close to the dive boats. Potato cods, which are a rare type of large grouper, Napoleon wrasses, king mackerel, large tuna, and gray reef sharks are all candidates for coming around at this dive site.

Large coral heads and fish life are seen all over the reef. At the southwest end of the reef, big bumphead parrotfish occasionally are observed chomping on large pieces of coral.

Big sponges are the norm here, large enough to form an easy chair for a man. Around the scattered sponges are corals that have leaf fish, which are very well camouflaged and sway in the surge like a real piece of fallen flora. There is also a small channel reef that splits off from the main reef. It has a great fish population and some nice hard corals and gorgonians.

Heading down to the east end, garden eels sway gently with the current, picking out nutrients as they protrude from their homes in the sea floor. Divers must approach them slowly and breath very lightly, as bubbles and quick movements will cause them to disappear.

Location:	Northwest Bali
Attractions:	Reef formations, schooling fish
Depth:	20 to 130 feet
Logistics:	Boat dive
Level:	Advanced, expert

A 20-minute boat ride away from the Reef Seen, the trip takes you along the Pemuteran coast. This reef is worth the trip if you like beautiful coral, sea fans, and invertebrate formations. Sliding into the water while looking west to the silhouetted triple volcanoes of Java lends an exotic air to this dive site. The south end of reef at can slope gently to 130 feet to a sandy bottom in a channel.

This nearly rectangular-shaped reef has scattered coral growth all over. The southern area is full of varied sea fans, soft corals, sponges, and pastel invertebrates like long-armed crinoids heavily woven together. Thick and healthy from feeding in the currents, many with

Crinoids

Crinoids are wiry but beautiful invertebrates found all over the Bali and Indo-Pacific region. These creatures are called spiders of the sea. Crinoids are very old animals, dating back millions of years. They come in a great variety of colors and have very different habits. Some are out during the day, hanging on sea fans to catch nutrients from the water. They are seen all over the reefs of Bali and the Indo-Pacific, where there are more than 90 recorded species. Others come out only at night, perching atop corals in a current to feed. Some are very reclusive, hiding quickly when they see a diver's light. And some are multi-colored, producing a striking image like that created by impressionist artists.

Immense barrel sponges grow on the reef at Lebar. ▶

The southern area of Lebar Reef is full of varied sea fans and accompanying crinoids.

sponges at their bases, these gorgonians come in an incredible variety of colors and shapes. Some are highlighted by fluffy soft corals that defy description for unique coloration. One especially impressive formation has a peach hue.

Small schools of jacks and fusiliers come by from out of the blue. In the upper areas around 60 feet, garden outcrops of tube sponges, soft carpets of sponges, and soft corals combine to create oases of seascaped beauty.

The top of the reef is thick in multi-colored staghorn corals and alive with absolute clouds of golden, blue, and silver chromis. This creates an incredible shallow reef show where fish surround the diver in swirls of motion and color.

The invertebrate life here can be very good, too.

Temple Wall 13

Location:	Northwest Bali
Attractions:	Platter corals, sponges
Depth:	10 to 100 feet
Logistics:	Boat dive
Level:	All levels

Located in front of a Balinese hilltop temple that overlooks the bay and the Bali sunrise on one side, and the clouded volcanoes of eastern Java on the other, this wall is full of surprises. The wall starts at about ten feet or less depending on the tide and drops down past 90 feet in some places, giving way to a sandy bottom and scattered hard coral heads adorned with fans and the ever-present barrel sponges.

Small lobsters, varied nudibranchs, flatworms, and pipefish all are in abundance on this prolific reef.

Siltation is a little heavy here, but this is good for the gorgonian and sea fan population. Beautiful pockets and small crevices in the reef are decorated by varied sponge life, black coral, wild wire corals, sea fans, and

The Giant Clam Mountain can be viewed from Pemuteran Bay.

Gorgonian sea fans and baitfish swarm a diver at Temple Wall.

other invertebrates, including scalloped oysters. Some sites with layered sea fans become shelter to lionfish, small baitfish, and brilliant damsels.

In the shallower water, varied coral species grow, including large razors that are found along the sandy rubble. Napoleon wrasse and jacks come here to forage among the scattered large coral heads.

Small flatworms and reef fish hang around the large coral heads, called bommies in this part of the world. This is a good place to find critters like eggshell cowries and an occasional fluted oyster.

Temple Wall makes an excellent night dive, as the invertebrate life along the wall is profuse. At night, all kinds of creatures come out or unfold, creating an incredibly colorful explosion everywhere the diver's light points. Look for basket stars and amazing crinoids.

Location:	Northwest Bali
Attractions:	Coral gardens, tropicals
Depth:	10 to 80 feet
Logistics:	Boat dive
Level:	All levels

Kebun Batu means "rock gardens," and it is a dropoff that can be reached from the Reef Seen beach. This is a pretty dive by day with lots of cabbage corals growing one atop the other for a beautiful layered effect.

It is a great night dive, especially if you're into small and unusual invertebrates. Along a walled coral head that drops to about 50 feet, camouflage spider crabs resemble debris as they blend into the background of an ascidian-covered orange sponge. Shrimp, lobsters, slipper lobsters, tiny hermits, and large reef crabs are prolific. On one dive, a prehistoric-looking spongehead crab, a large crab that had adopted a two-foot sponge, and a Neanderthal spider crab that defies description were observed. Ringed pipefish with dazzling red-and-white markings are in the cabbage coral. Plurobranchs small and large, animals similar to nudibranchs but without the flowing gills, are seen in sizes much larger than those described by most biology books. Their unique patterns and accompanying shrimp make them great abstract studies. Add some unusual tube worms, feather dusters, and a large purple-tipped sea anemone with a brilliant orange clown anemonefish (at only 10 feet), and you have an interesting snorkel or dive good for hours of undersea pleasure.

A tiny shrimp rides an unusually large plurobranch.

Location: Northwest Bali
Attractions: Invertebrates, night diving
Depth: 10 to 60 feet
Logistics: Boat dive
Level: Snorkel, novice, advanced, expert

This reef is a brief snorkel from the front of the aquatic center. It is good for snorkeling, introductory dives, a last shallow dive of the day, and an easy night dive. Meaning "Chris' Garden," this reef can slope down to 60

A wrasse hovers over a barrel sponge at Kebun Chris.

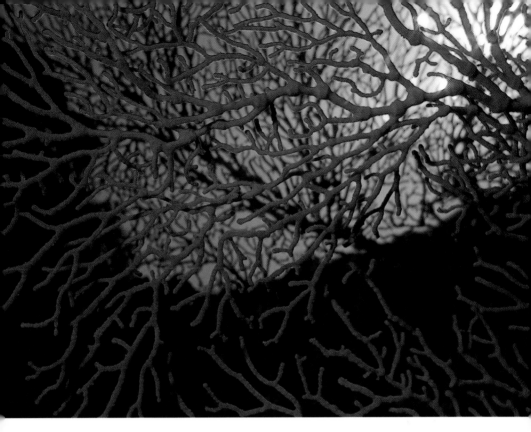

Delicate sea fans are highlighted by the sun.

feet, with various porites and acropora corals comprising the bulk of the growth here.

At night, small and large crinoids climb out on top of the coral heads to catch food in the current. They make excellent macrophotography subjects. Beautiful anemone hermit crabs scour the sandy sea floor looking for a morsel to eat, their shells covered with dazzling white sea anemones. A variety of eels, glass and cleaner shrimp, crabs, and nudibranchs are seen coming out of this reef area at night.

Juvenile lionfish, stonefish and cardinalfish are all found along the coral heads. They make great macrophotography subjects, too, as they fit well into a framer and will usually hold still when stunned by the diver's light. Look out for their dorsal spines, however: Though small, they can still give a painful sting.

At least four different types of pipefish are found here. Sea pens only two inches long grow from the sand right under the boat anchorage and only come out at night. Enjoy a long, leisurely shallow dive here, especially at night, for a good look at Indo-Pacific invertebrates.

Part of the reef is regrowing after being damaged, so take care with your fins not to dislodge the new corals and sponges that are trying to rebuild in the rubble.

Menjangen North   16

Location:	Western Bali
Attractions:	Wall, pelagic fish, big fans
Depth:	10 to 130 feet
Logistics:	Shore dive
Level:	All levels

Heavily wooded and populated by monkeys and exotic and rare birds, Menjangen means "deer" in Balinese. The deer of the park swim the narrow channel to graze on Menjangen Island, which is highlighted by sheer dropoffs on one side and beautiful slopes on the other.

This is one of the most beautiful underwater parks in the world. The Menjangen Dropoff has been compared in beauty to those found in Palau and the Great Barrier Reef. Divers are greeted by large batfish, who are used to seeing divers and come in close.

Menjangen Park offers a colorful dropoff in shallow water.

Whip corals grow along the Menjangen Park wall.

Other schools aren't quite as curious but swim the length of the reef past the pristine gorgonian sea fans, large elephant ear sponges, and glorious soft corals that line the reef from top to bottom. The drift diving here is excellent. Little effort is needed to cover a lot of distance along the dropoff.

At the top of the reef, a great variety of fish give flash and color to the reeftop. Where the currents flow, the fish like to gather because of all the nutrients brought in. Large groups of jacks form fast, exciting, and silvery schools. The top of the reef is full of basslets. Their orange and gold colors make Indonesian reefs a kaleidoscope.

Location:	Western Bali
Attractions:	Anemones, sea fans
Depth:	10 to 120 feet
Logistics:	Shore dive
Level:	All levels

Menjangen South is a turn to the right at the cut on the east side of the island. The familiar batfish will be there to greet you, but the terrain will start looking a little different quite soon. The dropoff is not quite as sheer as that along the popular northern wall: It is more gradual and there is a white sand bottom.

The clownfish looks like it is exploding from this Bali anemone.

Copper Sweepers line the reef at the Menjangen Channel.

The reeftop is alive with tropicals like basslets and chromis and schools of sergeant majors and staghorn damsels. There is also a good variety of anemones and various clownfish, from the percula to the tomato clown, in 30 feet of water or less. There are also developing platter corals that have juvenile chromis hovering close and then disappearing into the branches.

Prior to the time the reef was designated protected, some dynamite fishing took place. The reef has rebounded reasonably well. The best diving is 80 feet and above, with lots of sea fans and sea whips to peruse. There is also a great diversity of angelfish here, and they are fairly tame and can be photographed with patience and the proper approach.

There is much less of a current here than along the north site, making macrophotography possible with very little effort involved.

Listen for sounds in the water that may alert you to schooling dolphins. As this is near the pass, they have been known to accompany dive boats to and from this site.

Location:	Western Bali
Attractions:	Coral heads, sandy flats
Depth:	25 to 80 feet
Logistics:	Boat dive
Level:	Advanced, expert

This reef area has some of the brightest white sand in Indonesia, and there are large coral heads sticking up like Mardi Gras Medusas. Diving here can be long and relaxed as most of the time the bottom never gets deeper than 60 feet. Look around each large coral head for small invertebrate life like tunicate colonies that come in a variety of shapes, sizes, and colors.

There is one immense elephant ear sponge here that is bright orange and well over six feet high with lots of tunicates growing on the side that faces the current. The sponge life is varied and quite colorful all around this unique site.

The usual game plan is to ride whatever current there might be, doing a drift dive around the southwest point. This takes the diver past varied terrain and through channels that produce eagle rays, mantas, and occasional dolphins.

Look for extremely large star puffers here, exceeding two feet in length. They like to munch on starfish. There are also batfish here that have probably been fed by dive guides. They will follow you for a mile or more, hoping for a handout.

A huge bright orange elephant ear sponge is covered with colonies of tunicates in the Menjangen Channel.

Location:	Western Menjangen Island
Attractions:	Sea whips, soft coral formations
Depth:	10 to 130 feet
Logistics:	Boat dive
Level:	All levels

The popular dive sites at Menjangen are the east walls, but these coral gardens and slopes to the west, where the boat parks in sight of the majestic volcanic peaks of Java, are great for diving as well. The dives start at the reeftop in 20 feet or so of water. Many entry points have a sandy bottom that spills over into the plains of soft, flowing corals. The wall and dropoff can be steep or gentle slopes that are covered with sea fans and unique invertebrate life.

The sea fan colors range from deep forest greens to blood red, with all kinds of variations. This wall can get quite steep at times. In other places, there are canyons and crevices. Although it is possible to make a deep dive here, I suggest cruising at about 50 or 60 feet to take in the most of the underwater world.

There is a deep wreck along the reef. I'm told it is probably Dutch in origin and was sunk during the Japanese wartime occupation of the Indonesian islands. Bottles and some other artifacts have been taken from the wreck, but it is within the marine reserve and should not be pilfered so other divers can enjoy this rusting gem. Part of it is well beyond the recommended safe diving limits and there are no chambers nearby, so use your head if you want to have a look.

Cotton candy coral decorates a sponge at the preserve near Java.

Location:	Orote Peninsula
Attractions:	Cavern, sea whips, fish
Depth:	25 to 35 feet
Logistics:	Boat dive
Level:	All levels

On Bali Hai Cruises, which leave daily from Benoa Harbor in southeast Bali, all kinds of people mingle. The cruise goes over to Nusa Lembongan, a small island with a population of fishermen. People on the cruise can swim, go for water rides, eat, or just relax. Divers get a briefing on board so they know what is in store for them.

Many venture onto the island, which has only a couple of small hotels. One of the most eclectic is Waka Nusa Resort. The rooms of this sandy retreat are patterned after traditional Indonesian homes to the east of the islands. Their high ceilings keep them cool, and avante garde decor makes them unique. A refreshing blue pool is irresistible.

Soft corals and feather stars intertwine at the preserve.

Ocean sunfish are rarely seen on the reef, but come in close at Lembongan at certain times of the year.

Beneath the mooring for the Bali Hai vessel, a marine park has been established. Only 30 feet deep, markers take the diver around to different reef sites. Lionfish are at one spot, and flowing sea anemones and their clownfish at another. There are clouds of fish that hang under the mooring for feeding from curious snorkelers. This is a pleasant dive for those unfamiliar with Indonesian waters or for those on a day trip wanting to learn a little more about the sea.

Location:	Lembongan Bay
Attractions:	Incredible variety of ocean life, wild currents
Depth:	25 to 130 feet
Logistics:	Boat dive
Level:	Advanced with guide, expert

Don't try this at home!

Want to take a wild ride? Just step into the water off Lembongan Island in the Bali Straights and hang onto your mask, fins, and regulator. This trip isn't for everyone. The divers of Bali Hai cruises call it adrenaline diving, and it is really an awesome rush.

Strong tidal and inter-island currents along these flats about 60 feet down make the waters unpredictable. One hour they'll be calm and unmoving; an hour later, a seven-knot blast grabs the diver for the ride of a lifetime. Down and up currents and upwellings from deep below all add to the excitement of this amazing, full-speed roller coaster ride. Add occasional temperature changes of 20 degrees, and this dive has a chilling effect unmatched anywhere in the world.

These flats lead to a ledgy country called the Blue Corner. In this wild environment, rays can be found hovering. Flying full force into a school of large black stingrays can be a real eye-opener! These rays are normal-

Feeding in the consistent current, sea anemones cover the coral heads.

Large black rays are found at the Lembongan Blue Corner.

ly observed buried in the sand, but like to hover above when the current cooks, presumably catching food as the water whisks it by. If they are found on calmer days, they can be roused from the sand. But care has to be taken when observing these rays as one flick of a tail will inflict a nasty puncture.

The Lembongan Blue Corner is an interesting site that offers sharks on occasion and other denizens of the deep. But by far, the most fascinating animal to see is the mola-mola, or ocean sunfish.

This fish looks like nothing else. Its tiny mouth, huge dorsal fins, minimal tail, and set-back eyes make you wonder what God was thinking when creating the ocean sunfish. These animals are rarely seen near the coral reef, preferring to drift with the ocean currents in pursuit of their favorite food, the purple jellyfish. The mola-mola come near the reef for a brief time, presumably to mate. At this time, clouds of bannerfish and even French angels come to clean the parasites from their bizarre bodies.

They come into the reefs of Lembongan Island, a tiny and hilly spit across the Bali Strait. In these wild and cold waters, they mate and experience the reef for a few brief weeks during late August and early September. They stay in an area swept by unpredictable currents and punctuated by cold ocean upwellings that make this one of the wildest dives on earth. Add to the action giant black stingrays that float above huge sandy valleys, and you have a dive site that is like going into wildest Africa. And you may never want the norm again after experiencing an adrenaline ride that takes you whisking through the sea to perhaps glimpse a giant sunfish.

Mola-Mola or Ocean Sunfish

The Lembongan Blue Corner is an interesting area that offers big sharks on occasion and other denizens of the deep. But by far, the most fascinating animal to see is the mola-mola, or ocean sunfish.

These incredibly odd creatures look like nothing else in the sea. A stalker in the drifting world of the open ocean, they represent the very top of the food chain in a vagrant world of plankton that lives just below the surface of the ocean. Using their huge dorsal and anal fins, they glide through dense layers of tiny animals eating at will or looking for their favorite food, the purple jellyfish. Their tiny mouths and bony flap of tough skin don't lend themselves to a large animal, but the mola can reach a size of ten feet in height and weigh over a ton. Their eye sits far back away from their mouths so the stinging tentacles of jellyfish can't harm them.

They show up in Lembongan waters during August and September. No one knows for sure why they come, but local divers see them in pairs in this area, suggesting mating activity.

They hang vertically in the water along the dropoffs, being cleaned by big schools of bannerfish. Even a regal angelfish occasionally gets into the action. Their skins are full of parasites that make fine meals for other fish. Their thick skin covers a body made up mostly of cartilage.

Ocean sunfish don't seem to be too afraid of divers. It is likely they don't see divers very often as they drift in the open sea following the movement of plankton.

◄ *Tiny baitfish break the water off the Lembongan Straits.*

Unusual rock island at Nusa Penida cliffline. ►

Location:	Nusa Penida
Attractions:	Breathtaking coral gardens
Depth:	20 to 90 feet
Logistics:	Boat dive
Level:	All levels

The reefs surrounding Lembongan have seen little in the way of divers or fishermen. For this reason, the coral gardens are world class. The profusion of life is incredible.

Here, you might see a sea snake. Beautiful to watch as it winds its way through the corals, it is easy to forget that it is highly poisonous. But its mellow personality means that divers are rarely at risk from a sea snake bite. The true clownfish is found in the anemones along the reef. Bright orange and full of energy, these little guys will battle awesome currents to stake their place in the anemone's tentacles.

It doesn't seem possible, but the reeftop is even more alive than the reefs of the north. Cloud after cloud of basslets and chromis form a layer over the corals that is a tribute to the beauty of the underwater world.

There are few reefs in the world to match the dive site known simply as S.D. Big sponges grow everywhere, with crinoids or sea spiders fighting for space at their lips. Platter corals grow high and wide. Anemones live in groups, feeding on the nutrients brought in by the inter-island currents.

Pygmy copper sweepers move like clouds at S.D.

Mangrove Point 23

Location:	North Lembongan Island
Attractions:	Fish life, large sponges
Depth:	10 to 130 feet
Logistics:	Boat dive, knowledgeable guide
Level:	Snorkel, novice, advanced, expert

This site is divemaster Chuat Wullur's favorite spot to take all levels of divers coming into the Waka Nusa Resort to see the island's waters. Shal-

A starfish moves across a soft coral.

The currents at Mangrove Point twist coral and sponge growth into wild shapes.

low snorkels, novice diving in 20-foot depths, and also magnificent current rides for the experienced can all be found along this reef.

Typically, the current carries divers to the south and a dive starts at the tip, near a mangrove stand that runs along the coast. The currents are normally pretty calm until 35 to 40 foot depths are reached. Divers can catch the flow and coast over big barrel sponges, sea fans and lots of fish.

Around 70 to 80 feet, small schools of sweetlips can be seen flashing their bright yellow bodies in a symmetrical formation. Keep an eye out into the blue: Dogtooth tuna will come into view and an occasional whitetip shark also makes an appearance.

The most fish action can be seen along the tip and the sloping wall at somewhat deeper depths. Look at the odd shapes of the sponges and corals as they are attached and formed in the currents.

There are some huge angelfish on this reef. Colorful juvenile regal angelfish, stealthy yellowmask angels, striking blue-ringed angels, and some very big emperor angelfish are all found in the coral bommies. This place is a fish photographers paradise.

There is coral damage to the south where villagers removed the coral to make plots for their seaweed farms, but it is coming back slowly in some places.

A diver spots a moray eel at Mangrove Point.

Location:	Nusa Penida
Attractions:	Sloping reefs, big coral heads
Depth:	20 to 110 feet
Logistics:	Boat dive, experienced guide
Level:	Snorkel, novice, advanced, expert

This dive can be enjoyed by all levels of diver, as much of the dive area is protected and relatively shallow. The bay has two entrances, and a large rock sits in the center. If diving along here, currents can be strong and divers can be swept out along the outside wall, which can be very tricky diving. This is why an experienced guide is needed, so a disoriented diver doesn't take the wrong turn and wind up being swept away. But inner Crystal Bay is pretty tame and has some splendid coral formations and marine life. There are very large bommies, that are havens for marine life. Large schools of glass sweepers form living walls under many overhangs. Look at the brilliant orange soft corals that form here and the bottom-ori-

A purple-rimmed table coral at Crystal Bay makes a colorful backdrop for a starfish.

Striped catfish swirl into a ball formation at Crystal Bay.

ented basslets that swim upside down. I have seen extremely large angelfish and a monster eel exploring these. There is also one with a bloody big hole in it that forms a small cave that divers can carefully swim through.

There is an incredible amount of soft leather coral growth in this bay. Water temperatures tend to be a little cool, and this coral must thrive on those conditions. In one area, the large coral ears are packed together over a broad expanse, carpeting the sea floor.

When near the dropoff, look for larger creatures like eagle rays, dog-tooth tuna, sharks, and an occasional bumphead wrasse. Schooling surgeonfish are abundant in some spots.

There is a lone monster clam shell from a tridacna gigas that was poached long ago. Close to this shell is a major sand patch that can produce surprises to the observant diver, like a ball of striped catfish.

Location:	Nusa Penida Western Cliffline
Attractions:	Manta rays, rocky with varied life
Depth:	10 to 70 feet
Logistics:	Boat dive, local guide
Level:	Snorkel, novice, advanced, expert

Given the proper sea conditions, Manta Point can be enjoyed by all levels of divers, including snorkelers who can watch giant devilfish coast gracefully below them. During certain times of the year, groups of manta rays gather at the reef area surrounding this large rock to visit the cleaning stations, mate, have young, and do all those things manta rays do, like feed-floating into the current with their immense mouths open.

One of the most incredible displays I've ever seen in the sea took place one mid-morning in April. The day itself was magical. Accompanied by Lembongan explorer Mike Cortenbach, Chuat Surjaya from Waka Nusa Resort, and Stefanie Sager from *Pacific Below* magazine, we left Waka Nusa Resort after sunrise. The sea was like glass as we headed out. Clouds of silvery baitfish broke the surface in a huge "shoosh" and then returned to the sea, leaving tiny ripples on the water.

Snorkeling with a manta at Manta Point.

A manta swims by a cleaning station at Manta Point. ▶

The eerie coastline of Nusa Penida West towers straight up from the sea. Waterfalls and rugged walls gradated through time lend a medieval cast to this no man's land. Along the coast is an amazing manmade passage along a sheer wall. This walk to doomsday is fashioned from bamboo and leads from the very top of the cliff face in a zigzag fashion to a small temple in front of a flowing freshwater fall along the pounding surfline. The water cascades out of the mount along a rounded rock and into the sea. Caves have formed on both sides of the rocky outfall. When approached in the early morning and the boat engine is shut off, the falls seem to be emitting a chant. Beautiful and haunting, this music carries across the ocean and dissipates past the horizon.

People from the village above make the treacherous trek down 500 feet of sheer cliff to get water daily. The arid features of the plateau above make it necessary for these hearty yet isolated people to traverse the steep face as part of their daily regimen of survival on Nusa Penida.

Manta Point is a large rock next to a smaller outer rock along this wild cliffline. The rocks are home to fruit bats, flying mammals resembling small foxes, that roost on the islands by day and fly to the mainland at night to forage for fruit and other edibles. Their passage at dusk looks like Mother Nature's version of a Dracula movie.

Diving is done in the shallow channel and around the boulders of this site. It was here that the sea revealed some of her many secrets. After a dive where we spotted at least eight of the rays, either solitary or in pairs, visiting a series of cleaning stations at the point, we got back on the boat. While preparing to plan for a second dive, we spotted the dorsal fins or wing tips of a few mantas coming out of the water.

After taking a closer look, we realized that there were not just a few, but dozens of rays in the water. They were literally lined up in a long parade around the outer edges of the rocks, many of them breaking the surface and slapping the water with their wings. They were big and small and col-

Manta rays feed from the surface at Manta Point. ▶

◀ *Clouds of pygmy sweepers sparkle under a coral head at Nusa Penida.*

ored in the spectrum of everything from light gray with brilliant white underbellies to jet black with just a speck of white on the mandibles.

We entered the water on snorkel and found them in groups of six and more, swimming in circles, doing somersaults, and generally having a wild time. There were very small, young rays, pregnant females, and very large, ocean-going mantas. Most were at the surface but many were also 10 to 20 feet underneath us. Some would swim away, but others would come right at us, mouths agape feeding on planktonic matter. We touched some and some touched us. It was an absolutely incredible interaction with some of the largest, most graceful and powerful creatures of the sea. Not a lot is really known about manta rays. Biologists think this follow-the-leader, rolling, tumbling, showing-off behavior is some sort of mating game. The mantas know for sure, but whatever it is, it is truly an awesome spectacle. We spent at least an hour and a half with them until they had basically worn us out. They dispersed and continued to feed below us. We came back from a karmic experience never to be forgotten.

A spotting like this cannot be guaranteed every day at Manta Point, but they are consistently seen at the nearby cleaning stations when the season is right. Because the coast is not always hospitable, their exact pattern isn't known, but the months of December through March seem to be the most consistent for manta ray spottings.

There is a "flyway" of sorts that they follow, sort of like deer on a forest trail. They will come in along this invisible path, normally into the current, and hover over a series of cleaning stations. Look for the small cleaner wrasse and butterflyfish that like to preen these animals.

The mantas can be calm or skittish, depending on the day and the manta. Wait in the vicinity and don't chase or try to ride them. Breathe as lightly as possible. The curious ones will come by for a look. Watch their power and technique. Ocean worshipper David Doubilet once told me that there is nothing in the sea that looks like a manta ray. Nothing compares to their form either. They have given people cause to call manta encounters a religious experience.

If you are lucky, Manta Point may be the place you are able to say your encounter with this marvelous sea creature gave you just such a feeling.

◄ Manta rays allow snorkelers to join them as they feed and perform mating rituals at Manta Point.

3

East of Bali

The islands to the east of Bali are varied and little-explored by touring travelers. The best way to visit them is on some sort of live-aboard vessel where you can dive, sail, and explore this unique area. They are basically the islands of central Indonesia, and their region is called Nusa Tengarra. The cultures here are rich and varied. In places like Sumba, westerners are rarely seen and will be greeted with odd looks and comments. Many islands have animist tribes, people who traditionally worship animals. The odd monuments and graves alone are worth a day trip.

Komodo dragons are the last living dinosaurs, a remnant of the Jurassic period.

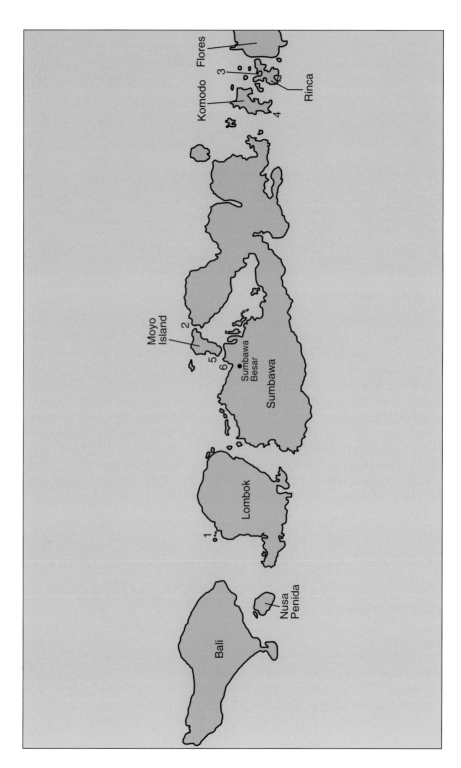

67

A Komodo dragon basks in the morning sunlight.

You may have to get out an atlas for this section, as there are names here few people have heard of in geography class. Many are found only on maritime charts. But a visit to this relatively unknown area is well worth the time and exploration.

It is here you find the remnants of the Jurassiac Period, the Komodo dragons. These giant monitor lizards eat everything they see, including deer, man, and themselves. The trip to one of the reserves at Komodo or Rinca is worth it, but stay with a guide. Those who have wandered off alone have become local legends and lessons in what not to do. These giants do swim and can dive to 30 feet. This is a very rare happening, however, so if you see one underwater consider yourself fortunate.

Dive Site Ratings

	Snorkel	Novice	Advanced	Master
East of Bali				
1 Lombok's Gilis	x	x	x	x
2 Satonda	x	x	x	x
3 Rinca		x	x	x
4 Komodo's Toro Lia Rock	x	x	x	x
5 Sandy Shoals	x	x	x	x
6 Moyo Dropoff			x	x

Location:	Northwestern Lombok, Gili Air, and Gili Trawangan
Attractions:	Varied terrain, surprising fish life
Depth:	20 to 90 feet
Logistics:	Boat dive
Level:	All levels

There are three islands just off Lombok's west coast that are a favorite haunt for day-trippers. The Gilis (Gili Air, Gili Trawangan, and Gili Meno) are low, sandy islands with shallow blue waters and nice beaches. Each has a restaurant or two and the usual T-shirt stands. There are some modest losmen and a hotel here, too.

Diving in the Gilis is pleasant, especially if you are into invertebrates. Off Gili Air, there is a nifty channel that allows a shallow and easy drift

---

Anemones

One of the most beautiful creatures of the sea is the anemone. Literally translated, it is a flower of the sea.

The waters of Bali are the home of a wide variety of sea anemones. The beautiful swaying of the sea anemone tentacles in the surge is similar to a graceful undersea ballet. Many anemones have small fish living with them. Dubbed clownfish, these unusual characters actually live together with the anemones, which is most closely related to corals, and they share an unusual life. In Bali, the true clownfish, *percula,* can be found, with its brilliant white and orange markings. Clownfish live within the stinging tentacles of the anemone, free from harm through a coating their body develops.

At night, the brilliant colors of the sea anemone are even more evident. Anemones probably continue their quest for food, as the dark doesn't hamper them. Their clownfish don't follow suit as it may be too visually demanding for them to find food in the dark.

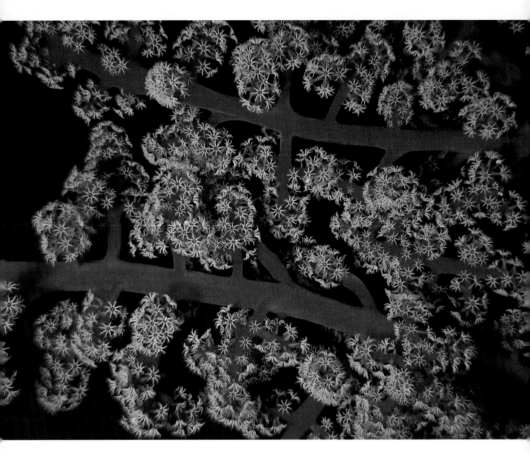

Cotton candy corals provide a coral close-up photo subject and can be found along the dropoffs in Nusa Tengarra.

dive. The slope is sandy with patch coral and flowing soft corals. Sea anemones are common with the cantankerous percula clownfish. There are a couple of local fish traps planted here that are made of bamboo. While the "free Willy" spirit in us wants to break these things and allow the fish to be let go, we must remember that this is a food source for local families. Enjoy the drift here and stop when you see something of interest. The channel looks as though there should be something big swimming by occasionally, and whitetip sharks have been seen here, so keep an eye on the blue void. There are big elephant ear sponges as well.

The diving is even better off Gili Trawangan. To the north and west there is a rocky shoreline and a point. The area around the point can be

A traditional finisi passenger ship sits off the famous and rugged Komodo Island. ▶

Cuttlefish in the Gilis pose for videographers.

rough and churned up, but the sloping shelf nearby contains large coral heads, big patches of staghorn, and other acropora and occasional valleys that are home to fish schools. There are cuttlefish in abundance here and they can be approached quite closely. Watch as they react to you. They will change colors in a furious progression that ranges from a wild bioluminescent to stark pale. The boulders that are scattered around provide refuge for big snappers that weigh in the 80- to 100-pound range.

Satonda 2

Location:	Near Sumbawa
Attractions:	Sloping wall, sponges, coral
Depth:	10 to 100 feet
Logistics:	Boat or shore dive
Level:	All levels

The underwater sights here are rivaled by the land activity on this small reserve. Uninhabited, it sits off the wild west coast of Sumbawa. Diving along the south tip is protected most of the year and there are slopes with cascading corals. The coral stops at about 90 feet and gives way to a sandy, current-swept plain. Large barrel and elephant ear sponges are prevalent. The reeftop is pretty with lots of small tropicals giving it life

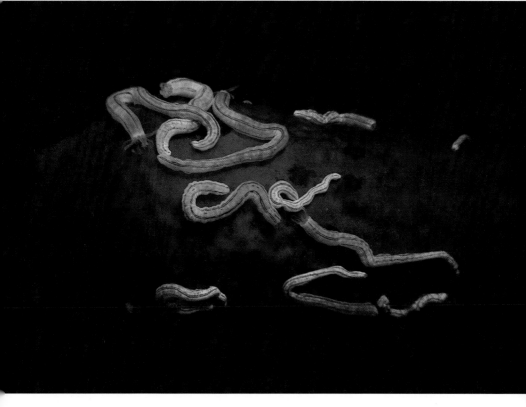

Small sea cucumbers move across a sponge.

A fruitbat colony lives on the nature preserve at Satonda.

and color. I have seen eagle rays here and large cuttlefish. This can be a relaxing dive at about 60 feet. One of the peskiest remoras I have ever encountered joined me for too long here. The undersea ballet I performed to rid myself of this black demon caused my dive buddy to nearly drown from laughter.

On land there is a fruitbat colony and a marine lake. The lake is pretty but has no special life in it. The bat colony is wild. Like a Dracula movie, these huge flying foxes hang upside down in trees by day. Their screeching can be heard miles out at sea, and there are thousands of them who come here to rest during the days and then fly eerily over the mainland to feed after dark.

Location:	Loho Kima Bay
Attractions:	Crinoids, anemones, thickets
Depth:	20 to 80 feet
Logistics:	Boat dive
Level:	Novice, advanced, expert

Cool, green, and bizarre, that's Loho Kima Bay. This is part of a national park in the Komodo chain that is surrounded by mangroves. The nutrients that run off the mangrove marsh provide a veritable smorgasbord for the invertebrate life in the shallow staghorn forests and sandy channels.

The variety of coloration is amazing. Crinoids in many hues of pastels stay in the acropora branches. There is an incredible number of sea anemones nestled around the island. Some hide in the sand when touched.

Fish Schools—Pygmy Sweepers

The sea is home to schools of fish that live in great numbers along the outer barrier reef. Sometimes they mingle, performing an odd ballet of friend and foe. Copper pygmy sweepers use the shelter of the coral heads and sponges, forming glistening walls of thousands of fish. This swirl of silver or copper attracts divers, and some predators as well. The pure fluid beauty of this fish school draws the human to its heart, engulfing and then sometimes fleeing in a rapid rush up the reef to start a new performance.

The rich waters off Rinca are green from nutrients from the mangroves.

At Rinca, mangroves turn the water green with nutrients that help crinoids and sponges thrive.

◄ *Multi-hued crinoids abound on the reefs in the Indo-Pacific.*

These can be toxic, so handle with care. Others are broad and colorful with percula clownfish and tiny shrimps nestled in the tentacles.

There are broad sponges and large coral formations scattered along the channels. Huge wire corals spiral off the bottom, and immense schools of pygmy copper sweepers hover over coral heads. Bizarre lettuce leaf coral and vase corals have formed in the current line. In one spot, the sea floor is covered with black urchins.

This is a great spot for macrophotography. A mantis shrimp living in some coral rubble was a colorful macro video subject here. It can be a little cool, so bring an extra dive skin to wear under your wetsuit.

Location: Panta Tana Mera
Attractions: Vast variety of sea life
Depth: 10 to 90 feet
Logistics: Boat dive
Level: All levels

There are few places in the world that pack more marine life into one small place than the reef at Toro Lia Rock. Located along an incredibly scenic bay on Komodo Island, this rock barely breaks the surface at high tide. Follow it on down and you'll find a treasure trove of beauty.

There are strange currents here that feed a wild variety of white soft corals, deep, red-veined corals, and large, broad leather corals. There are reef tropicals everywhere and lionfish in groups, hovering over the reef in broad daylight feeding on the pygmy sweepers that layer the reeftop.

Deeper down, the schools of Moorish idols, bannerfish, and bumphead parrotfish keep the activity level high. Above, powder blue tangs also school along with drums and snappers. Big fish like jacks and tuna come in and out.

The rock also is covered with gorgonians and an awesome amount of encrusting marine life that makes for great macro photography. I have never heard anyone complain about a dive here, even though it can be surgey and visibility can be low. These nutrient-rich green waters have so much excitement and action going on that it's easy to get carried away trying to take it all in, so keep an eye on your depth gauge and air supply.

Bali's great diversity is shown in its unusual marine life like these encrusting invertebrate marine worms, corals, and sponges.

Sandy Shoals   6

Location:	North of Sumbawa Besar
Attractions:	Big fans, big fish schools
Depth:	20 to 130 feet
Logistics:	Boat dive
Level:	All levels with guide

A series of shallow reefs has a shallow top and sloping sides that are covered with a variety of corals and sponges, lots of schooling tropicals, and a glimpse at some real pelagic action. Along this dropoff, whitetip sharks can frequently be seen. Especially at the southern tip, currents attract a lot of schooling fish action—bigeye trevally, dogtooth tuna, and bumphead wrasse.

There are schools of bannerfish that add a lot of color to the reef. Add lots of bluestripe fusiliers and brilliant aqua surgeonfish, and you've found a spot that lends a diver a backdrop for hours of photography.

Sea fans and other invertebrate life of this rich region make this a great reef for relaxed yet fascinating diving. Few people come here except for some super-rich international movie stars who pay big bucks to camp on the Sumbawa mainland.

Incredible hues of red are evident in this soft coral.

Location: Saleh Bay
Attractions: Sharp wall, active sea life
Depth: 35 to 130 feet
Logistics: Boat dive
Level: Advanced, expert

This dropoff is near the Sandy Shoals reefs. It is supposed to be the most famous dropoff in the area, and some say it is world class. Pelagic fish are most often spotted here, although, like nearby Sandy Shoals, they can appear at any time. It is not unusual to see whitetip sharks and big tuna, especially dogtooth, come by to see what you're stirring up. Look for the occasional manta ray and whale shark under the proper conditions, which can mean low visibility and a lot of plankton in the water.

The sponge life here is varied and beautiful, with the immense Indonesian barrel sponges making their presence known on the reef. The Moyo Drop is known for its deep crevices and cuts.

A sea cucumber moves along an encrusting sponge.

Laden with color, sponges, corals and crinoids all compete for space. ▶

Bright soft corals mingle with basslets at the Lembongan reefs.

4

Smart, Safe Diving

Currents

The currents in the Indonesian waters can range from non-existent to treacherous. Sites along the northern and northeastern coasts of Bali are generally not known to be problematic. The sites off east-central Bali, in the Lembongan waters, and in the Komodo Region are known to have currents that can range to 13 knots, forming strong whirlpools that can pull a diver down. Please do not attempt to dive in an unfamiliar area. A knowledgeable guide and boatman are important to have in some of the wilder, little-dived areas and those areas that attract large, pelagic creatures.

Also, after diving in Bali and when you are returning to your hotel, remember that some mountain roads can gain altitude quickly and go quite high. Take care not to dive too deep, as going up in altitude can cause a form of decompression sickness. The nearest recompression facility is in

A diver plays with a sea fan along Menjangen Wall.

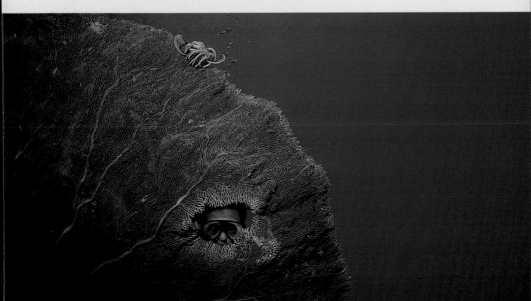

Java in Surabaya, an hour's flight from Denpasar. Better to be safe than sorry.

Dangerous Marine Animals

Bali boasts one of the most diverse fish and invertebrate populations in the world. The Indo-Pacific region is one of the ocean's richest areas. Night diving can be spectacular with a wide spectrum of color and a variety of odd and fascinating marine creatures coming into view. Few marine-related injuries are reported annually. Common sense and respect for wild animals goes a long way in preventing any sort of mishap on the reef.

Jellyfish. Jellyfish can be directed away from a diver by pushing them away by their bulbous top. Their lower sections and tentacles deliver the sting. Some people have mild reactions to jellyfish stings; others have severe allergic reactions. Normally, meat tenderizer will neutralize the sting of a jellyfish. See a physician for any problems.

Sea Urchins. These critters are the scourge of divers and swimmers worldwide. The victim normally kneels on or puts a hand or finger on an urchin. The animal's brittle spines break off and its puncture can be immediately painful. It usually takes a few weeks for the spines to work their way out. Antibiotic cream will keep the wound from infecting. For major punctures, see a physician.

Scorpionfish, Stonefish. These animals camouflage themselves easily, and injuries are also normally the result of an accidental meeting of diver and fish. These stings should not be taken lightly. Severe allergic reactions have occurred in some victims. See a doctor immediately or go to the emergency room at the hospital. Pain can sometimes be eased by submerging the wound in hot water.

Crown-of-thorns Starfish. The acanthaster can deliver a painful wound that can fester and become severely infected. Treat this wound at once and see a doctor. An old island cure is to put the mouth of the same animal that punctured you on the wound and it will suck out its poison. You can try this, but see a doctor too. The complications from a crown-of-thorns wound can be extensive if not treated properly.

Eels. Eels are normally shy and reclusive. Do not harass them or put your hand into any holes of the ship or the coral. Their teeth tilt backwards so they can deliver a wound that will shred skin.

Sharks. There are few documented cases of shark attacks on divers, and most of those involve some sort of spearfishing or something that gets a fish's blood in the water and excites a predator like a shark. The blood of a wounded fish will make sharks and barracudas competitive and aggressive. If a diver sees animals using this behavior, such as quick body movements or displays with their fins, he or she should leave the area and get out of the water.

Emergency Services

The only recompression chamber in the area is currently in Surabaya in Java, about an hour's flight from Bali. Efforts are being made to establish one in Bali. Ask your tour operator about the status of this chamber. For emergencies, have your hotel call the police and emergency services. The Indonesian name for pharmacy is *apotik* and the hospital is called a *rumah sakit.* Major medical care is normally done in Jakarta, but there is also a hospital in Denpasar.

Malarial problems are almost unknown in Bali but may be found in the islands east, as can some other maladies. Proper vaccination usually prevents any problems while on vacation. These islands are also without major medical facilities and recompression chambers. Check with a physician before leaving home to ensure you are properly vaccinated.

One Bali physician who deals with tourists is:

Dr. Jelantik
Jl. Hayam Wuruk
Sanur, Bali
Phone: 288466

Diver Guidelines for Protecting Fragile Marine Habitats

1. Maintain proper buoyancy control and avoid over-weighting.
2. Use correct weight belt position to stay horizontal, i.e., raise the belt above your waist to elevate your feet/fins, and move it lower toward your hips to lower them.
3. Use your tank position in the backpack as a balance weight, i.e., raise your backpack on the tank to lower your legs, and lower the backpack on the tank to raise your legs.
4. Watch for buoyancy changes during a dive trip. During the first couple of days, you'll probably breathe a little harder and need a bit more weight than the last few days.
5. Be careful about buoyancy loss at depth; the deeper you go the more your wet suit compresses, and the more buoyancy you lose.
6. Photographers must be extra careful. Cameras and equipment affect buoyancy. Changing f-stops, framing a subject, and maintaining position for a photo often conspire to prohibit the ideal "no-touch"

approach on a reef. So, when you must use "holdfasts," choose them intelligently.

7. Avoid full leg kicks when working close to the bottom and when leaving a photo scene. When you inadvertently kick something, stop kicking! Seems obvious, but some divers either semi-panic or are totally oblivious when they bump something.

8. When swimming in strong currents, be extra careful about leg kicks and handholds.

9. Attach dangling gauges, computer consoles, and octopus regulators. They are like miniature wrecking balls to a reef.

10. Never drop boat anchors onto a reef.

Diving Accidents

The Divers Alert Network (DAN), a membership association of individuals and organizations sharing a common interest in diving safety, operates a **24-hour national hotline (919) 684-8111** (collect calls are accepted in an emergency). DAN does not directly provide medical care; however, they do provide advice on early treatment, evacuation, and hyperbaric treatment of diving-related injuries. Additionally, DAN provides diving safety information to members to help prevent accidents. Membership is $10 a year, offering: the DAN *Underwater Diving Accident Manual,* describing symptoms and first aid for the major diving-related injuries and emergency room physician guidelines for drugs and i.v. fluids; a membership card listing diving-related symptoms on one side and DAN's emergency and non-emergency phone numbers on the other; 1 tank decal and 3 small equipment decals with DAN's logo and emergency number; and a newsletter, "Alert Diver," which describes diving medicine and safety information in layman's language, with articles for professionals, case histories, and medical questions related to diving. Special memberships for dive stores, dive clubs, and corporations are also available. The DAN Manual can be purchased for $4 from the Administrative Coordinator, National Diving Alert Network, Duke University Medical Center, Box 3823, Durham, NC 27710.

DAN divides the U.S. into 7 regions, each coordinated by a specialist in diving medicine who has access to the hyperbaric chambers in his region. Non-emergency or information calls are connected to the DAN office and information number, (919) 684-2948. The number can be dialed direct between 9 a.m. and 5 p.m. Monday–Friday Eastern Standard time. Divers should *not* call DAN for chamber locations. Chamber status changes frequently, making this kind of information dangerous if obsolete at the time of an emergency. Instead, divers should contact DAN as soon as a diving emergency is suspected. All divers should have comprehensive medical insurance and check to make sure that hyperbaric treatment and air ambulance services are covered internationally.

Diving is a safe sport and there are very few accidents compared to the number of divers and number of dives made each year. But when the infrequent injury does occur, DAN is ready to help. DAN, originally 100% federally funded, is now largely supported by the diving public. Membership in DAN or purchase of DAN manuals or decals provides divers with useful safety information and provides DAN with necessary operating funds. Donations to DAN are deductible as DAN is a legal non-profit public service organization.

The sandy beach along the western side of isolated Lembongan Island provides a scenic view of Mount Agung on Bali.

Appendix

The list below is included as a service to the reader. The author has made every effort to make this list complete at the time the book was printed. This list does not necessarily constitute an endorsement of these operators and dive shops. If operators/owners wish to be considered for inclusion in future reprints/editions, please contact Pisces Books, P.O. Box 2608, Houston, TX 77252-2608.

Dive Operators

Alam Anda (*Pike Travel*)
Jalan Legian Tengah 436N
Legian, Bali, Indonesia
Ph/FAX 62-361-752296

Bali Hai Cruises
Adrenaline Divers
P.O. Box 548
Denpasar, Bali, Indonesia
Ph: 62-361-734331
FAX 62-361-734334

Barrakuda Bali Dive
P.O. Box 1116
Nusa Dua, Bali, Indonesia
Ph: 62-361-772130
FAX 62-361-772131

Baruna Water Sports
P.O. Box 419
Kuta, Bali, Indonesia
Ph: 62-361-753809
FAX 62-361-752779

Calypso Bali Dive
P.O. Box 130
Amlapura, Candi Dasa, Bali,
Indonesia
Ph: 62-361-235536
FAX 62-361-235537

Dive & Dive's
Jalan I Gusti
Ngurah Rai No. 23
Sanur, Bali, Indonesia
Ph: 62-361-288052
FAX 62-361-289309

Dive Paradise Tulamben
P.O. Box 111
Amlapura, Tulamben, Bali, Indonesia

Ena Dive Centre
Jalan Pangenbak 07
Sanur, Bali, Indonesia
Ph/FAX 62-361-287945

Permai Dive Sport
Pantai Happy
Lovina, Singaraja, Bali, Indonesia
Ph: 62-362-23471

Reef Seen Aquatics
Attn: Chris Brown
Pondok Sari Beach Bungalows
Desa Pemuteran, Gerogkak,
Singaraja, Bali, Indonesia
Ph: 62-362-92339
FAX 62-362-92337

Spice Dive
P.O. Box 157
Singaraja, Bali, Indonesia
Ph: 62-361-23305

Stingray Dive Centre
P.O. Box 120 JKWB
Jakarta Pusat 10270, Indonesia
Ph/FAX: 62-362-570-0272

Tulamben Diving Centre
Tulamben, Amlapura, Bali, Indonesia

Yos Diving Centre
Jalan Ngurah Rai,
Tuban, Bali, Indonesia
Ph: 62-361-752005
FAX 62-361-752985

Boys frolic at the water temple in the hills overlooking the rice paddies at Tampaksiring.

Index